GEO
KIDS

Exploring The

WOODLAND

By
Holly Duhig

BookLife
PUBLISHING

©2019
BookLife Publishing
King's Lynn
Norfolk PE30 4LS
All rights reserved.
Printed in Malaysia.

A catalogue record for this book is available from the British Library.

ISBN: 978-1-78637-439-4

Written by:
Holly Duhig

Edited by:
Madeline Tyler

Designed by:
Gareth Liddington

CONTENTS

Words that look like **this** can be found in the glossary on page 24.

EXPLORING THE WOODLAND

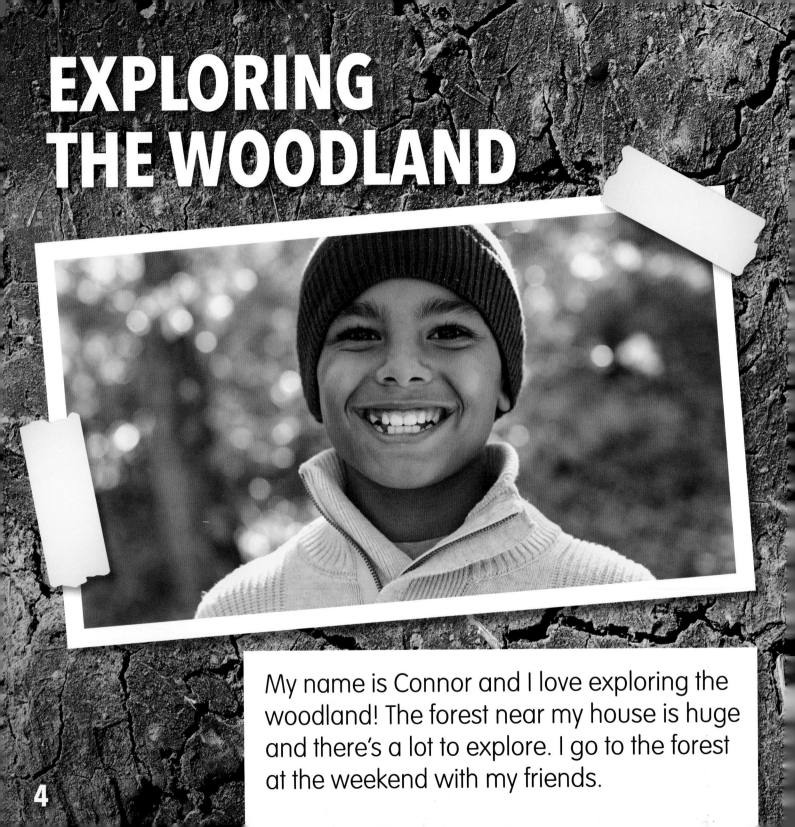

My name is Connor and I love exploring the woodland! The forest near my house is huge and there's a lot to explore. I go to the forest at the weekend with my friends.

I'm doing a project for school all about the forest, so I want to find out as much as I can about the forest **environment**. I'm going to keep notes as I explore.

GEO KIDS

Exploring The
WOODLAND

Connor Yates' Woodland Project

This is the forest near my house. The leaves are falling and turning orange: it's autumn!

TIMBER!

Sometimes there are fallen trees in the forest. They make great bridges for me and my friends. Sometimes you can see minibeasts like woodlice and ants crawling on them.

Fallen trees are often slippery! They might feel slimy and wet and have mushrooms growing out of the bark.

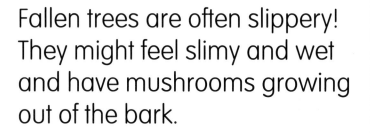

FALLEN TREES

Can you see this tree's roots?

Timber!

Sometimes trees fall because their roots are damaged by rot and mould or because of very windy weather. Roots keep trees in the ground – like an anchor. When they are weak or rotten, the tree might topple over.

After they fall, trees begin to rot. This puts nutrients into the soil around them. Mould and fungi help to break down dead trees. After this, insects and minibeasts can eat the rotting wood.

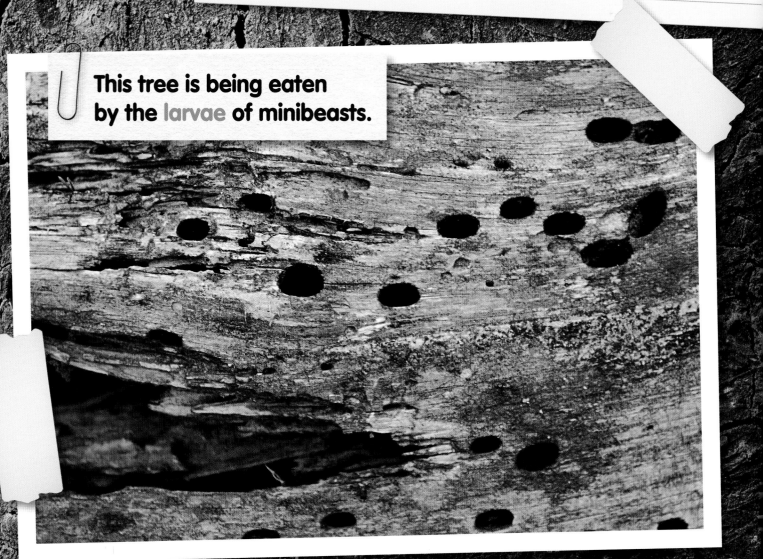

This tree is being eaten by the larvae of minibeasts.

DENS!

When we go to the forest, we like to make dens out of old tree branches. We prop the branches up around a tall tree and collect lots of smaller twigs and sticks to fill in the gaps.

We used branches from all sorts of trees to build our last den. I took the bark from some of the trees home with me so I could find out more about them. I was sad to leave our den behind, but hopefully some animals can use it after us.

Forest animals such as hedgehogs might use our den.

BARK AND BRANCHES

Silver Birch Bark

Pine Tree Bark

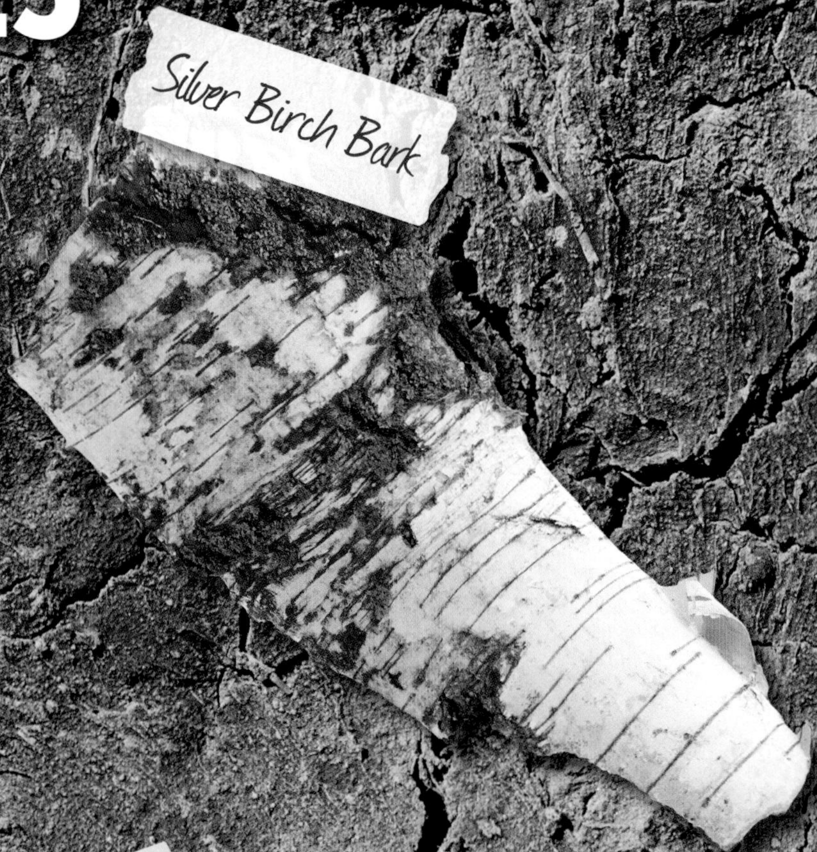

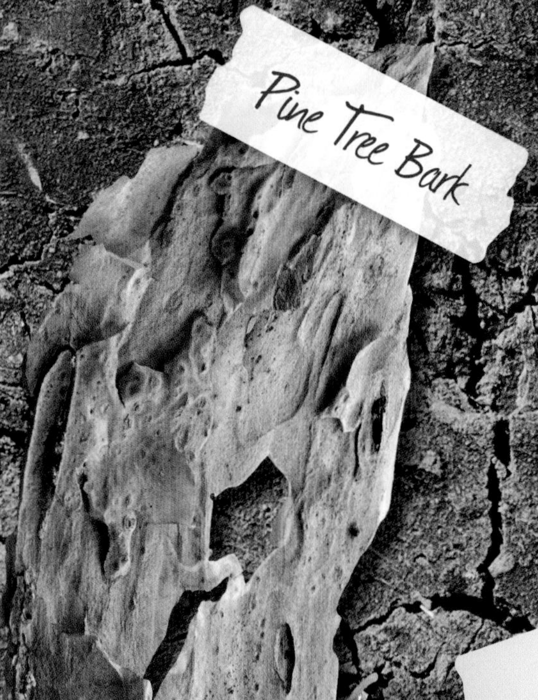

Bark is food for a lot of animals in the forest. Deer, rabbits and birds eat the bark of the birch tree.

As well as branches, I also found some tree stumps in the forest. You can learn a lot from a tree stump. The number of rings in a tree stump can tell you how many years old the tree is.

5 Years Old

9 Years Old

13

KAYAKING!

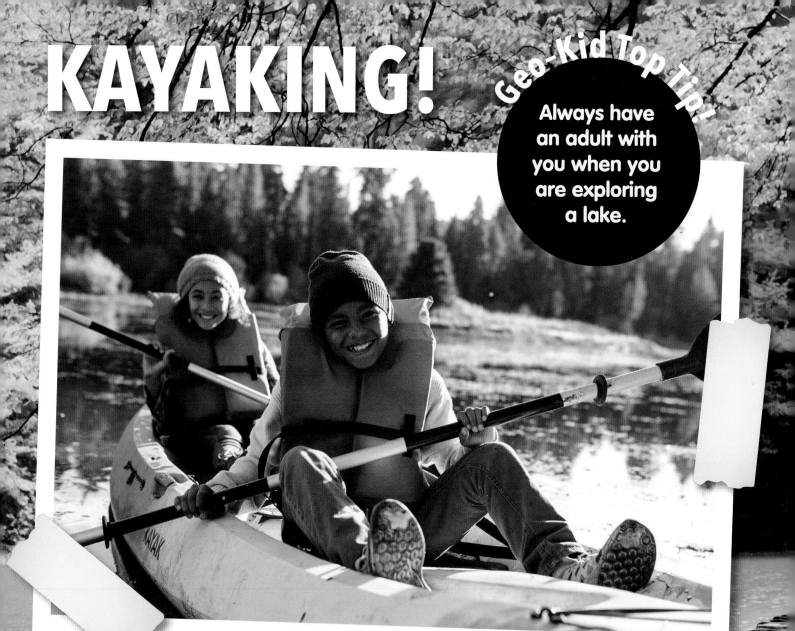

Geo-Kid Top Tip!

Always have an adult with you when you are exploring a lake.

Some forests have lakes in them. We like to go kayaking when we go to the forest. My sister and I share a kayak and we push ourselves along using the paddles.

14

When we go kayaking, we try to look out for fish. Splashes, ripples and bubbles on the surface of the water are often signs of fish.

FOREST LAKES

Some types of fish I have spotted in the lake include:

Pike

Carp

Eel

These fish are all freshwater fish. That means they live in freshwater lakes and rivers, rather than salty ocean water. Fish can breathe underwater using their gills.

The lake is also home to lots of ducks. You shouldn't feed ducks bread because it is not very good for them. When we feed the ducks, we feed them sweetcorn instead.

Drake

Ducks' feathers are waterproof!

Hen

JUMPING IN LEAVES!

Geo-Kid Top Tip! Watch out for any woodland creatures that might be hiding under piles of leaves.

My favourite thing about the forest in the autumn is jumping in the leaves! They make a great crunching sound!

The leaves are golden because it's autumn. You can make lots of fun things with autumn leaves. I always like to take some leaves home with me so I can make a **collage**.

TYPES OF TREES

The first leaf is from an oak tree. Oak trees can live for 1,000 years!

Elm Leaf

Maple Leaf

Oak Leaf

The lines in a leaf are actually its veins! They carry water and important minerals.

I learned that these trees all have leaves that turn brown and fall off in autumn. Trees that do this are called deciduous trees. Trees that keep their leaves all year round are called evergreens.

These trees are deciduous.

say: des-SID-dew-us!

These trees are evergreens.

LEAVING THE FOREST

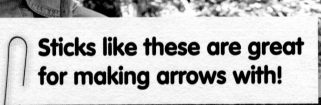

Sticks like these are great for making arrows with!

It's easy to get lost in a forest, so it's important to know how to get out. We made arrows in the ground with sticks wherever we went. Now all we have to do is follow the arrows back home.

You can also use a compass to find your way. When we went into the forest, our compass told us we were heading east. To get back home, we have to go west.

You could also use a GPS map on a smartphone or tablet.

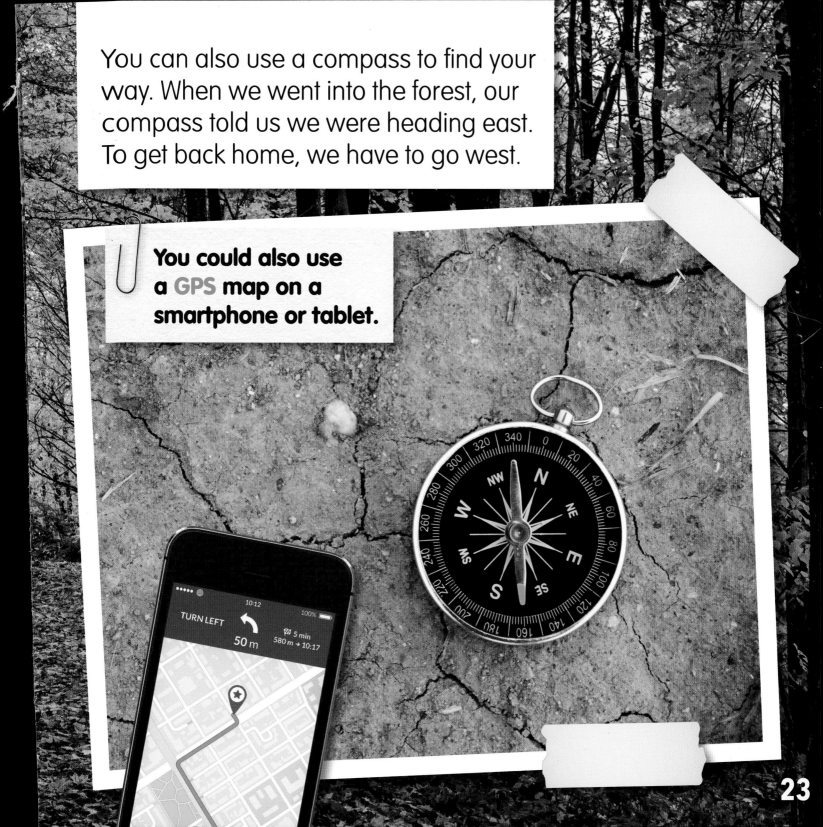

GLOSSARY

collage   a piece of art made by sticking different materials onto something

environment   the area in which a human, animal or plant lives

fungi   a type of life similar to plants but does not create food from sunlight; mushrooms yeast and moulds are fungi

gills   the organs that some animals use to breathe underwater

GPS   stands for global positioning system; a system that uses signals from satellites to find the location of something on a map

larvae   a type of young insect that must grow and change before it can reach its adult form

minerals   important things that plants, animals and humans need to grow

nutrients   natural substances that plants and animals need to grow and stay healthy

ridges   the long, narrow, raised parts of a surface

INDEX